BinaryCoder X

Developing Artificial intelligence

"To the relentless seekers of knowledge, the fearless pioneers of innovation, and the champions of ethical stewardship in the realm of artificial intelligence—this book is dedicated to you. May your curiosity inspire discovery, your ingenuity spark transformation, and your integrity guide the way forward. With deepest gratitude and admiration, BinaryCoder X."

"Unlock the mysteries, transcend the limits, and embrace the future of intelligence with 'Developing Artificial Intelligence' by BinaryCoder X. Welcome to the dawn of a new era."

BinaryCoder X

"To the relentless seekers of knowledge, the fearless pioneers of innovation, and the champions of ethical stewardship in the realm of artificial intelligence—this book is dedicated to you. May your curiosity inspire discovery, your ingenuity spark transformation, and your integrity guide the way forward. With deepest gratitude and admiration, BinaryCoder X."

"Unlock the mysteries, transcend the limits, and embrace the future of intelligence with 'Developing Artificial Intelligence' by BinaryCoder X. Welcome to the dawn of a new era."

BinaryCoder X

Contents

9.

10.

11.

Foreword

Foreword by BinaryCoder X:

In the ever-expanding universe of technology, few frontiers hold as much fascination and promise as artificial intelligence. As a coder, a thinker, and a seeker of knowledge, I've long been captivated by the boundless potential of AI to revolutionize our world. It is with great pleasure—and a sense of awe—that I introduce you to "Developing Artificial Intelligence."

This book is more than just a guide to the intricacies of AI development; it is a manifesto for the relentless pursuit of innovation and discovery. From the binary depths of machine learning algorithms to the ethereal heights of neural networks, "Developing Artificial Intelligence" invites you on a journey through the inner workings of the human mind and the digital realms of computational intelligence.

As a practitioner in the field of AI, I have witnessed firsthand the transformative power of intelligent machines to solve complex problems, automate tedious tasks, and augment human capabilities. But beyond the technical intricacies of AI lies a profound ethical imperative—a responsibility to ensure that our creations serve humanity with wisdom, compassion, and integrity.

In "Developing Artificial Intelligence," you will encounter not only the cutting-edge technologies and methodologies driving AI innovation but also the ethical considerations and societal implications that accompany the quest for artificial intelligence. Through a tapestry of anecdotes, case studies, and expert insights, this book illuminates the multifaceted landscape of AI development and challenges us to confront the ethical dilemmas and societal impact of our creations.

As we stand on the cusp of a new era defined by intelligent machines and digital cognition, "Developing Artificial Intelligence" serves as a beacon of inspiration and guidance for all those who dare to venture into the uncharted territory of AI exploration. Whether you are a seasoned AI practitioner, a curious novice, or a visionary leader shaping the future of technology, this book offers a captivating glimpse into the past, present, and future of artificial intelligence—and the profound implications it holds for humanity.

So, dear reader, I invite you to embark on this exhilarating odyssey through the realms of AI creation and discovery. Let us embrace the challenges, celebrate the triumphs, and chart a course towards a future where artificial intelligence serves as a force for good in the world.

Welcome to "Developing Artificial Intelligence." Welcome to the future.

With boundless curiosity and unwavering optimism,

BinaryCoder   X

Preface

Preface:

In the vast expanse of human ingenuity and ambition, there exists a frontier that beckons with the promise of untold possibilities and boundless innovation: the realm of artificial intelligence. "Developing Artificial Intelligence" invites you on a captivating journey through the labyrinthine pathways of AI creation, discovery, and transformation.

As we stand on the precipice of a new era defined by intelligent machines and digital cognition, the quest to develop artificial intelligence has captured the imagination of visionaries, scholars, and innovators alike. From the depths of research laboratories to the bustling corridors of tech startups, the pursuit of AI holds the potential to reshape our world in ways both profound and unforeseen.

In this evocative exploration, we delve into the heart of AI development, unraveling the mysteries of machine learning, neural networks, and computational intelligence. Through a tapestry of narratives, anecdotes, and insights from leading experts in the field, we uncover the intricacies of AI algorithms, the nuances of data science, and the ethical considerations that underpin the quest for artificial intelligence.

But "Developing Artificial Intelligence" is more than just a journey through the inner workings of algorithms and neural architectures—it is a testament to the human spirit of inquiry, innovation, and discovery. It is a celebration of the tireless pursuit of knowledge and the relentless quest to unlock the secrets of intelligence itself.

Join us as we embark on this exhilarating odyssey through the realms of AI creation and exploration. Whether you are a seasoned AI enthusiast, a curious novice, or a visionary leader shaping the future of technology, "Developing Artificial Intelligence" offers a captivating glimpse into the past, present, and future of AI—and the profound impact it holds for humanity.

Welcome to the frontier of artificial intelligence. Welcome to the journey of discovery. Welcome to "Developing Artificial Intelligence."

Let the adventure begin.

Warm regards,

[BinaryCoder   X]

Acknowledgement

1

Define The Objective

Title: Setting the Course: Defining Objectives in AI Development

—-

Welcome, seekers of knowledge, to the foundational cornerstone of artificial intelligence: Defining the Objective. Just as a sailor needs a clear destination before setting sail, so too does an AI project require a well-defined objective to navigate the vast sea of data and algorithms.

Imagine you're embarking on a journey to build an AI system. What is your destination? What problem do you seek to solve? This is where the journey begins.

1. The North Star:

Every successful AI project starts with a clear and precise objective, akin to a North Star guiding sailors through the night. Whether it's optimizing business processes, predicting customer behavior, or diagnosing diseases, the objective serves as the beacon illuminating the path forward.

2. Clarity Breeds Success:

A vague or ambiguous objective is like a compass spinning aimlessly, leading to wasted time, resources, and effort. By defining the objective with clarity and precision, you provide a roadmap for the entire project, guiding decision-making and prioritization at every turn.

3. Scope and Focus:

Defining the objective also helps delineate the scope of the project, allowing you to focus on what truly matters. It's tempting to try to solve every problem under the sun, but success often lies in narrowing your focus to a specific, achievable goal.

4. Measure of Success:

How will you know when you've reached your destination? By defining clear metrics and benchmarks upfront, you provide a yardstick against which to measure progress and success. Whether it's accuracy, efficiency, or customer satisfaction, these metrics serve as milestones on your journey.

5. Adaptability and Evolution:

While the objective provides direction, it's essential to remain adaptable in the face of uncertainty and change. As you embark on your AI journey, be prepared to course-correct, iterate, and evolve your objectives based on new insights and emerging challenges.

6. Ethical Considerations:

Lastly, but certainly not least, consider the ethical implications of your objective. How will your AI system impact society, privacy, and fairness? By integrating ethical considerations into the objective-setting process, you ensure that your AI journey is not only successful but also responsible and sustainable.

In conclusion, defining the objective is the crucial first step in any AI project. It serves as the guiding light, the compass, and the roadmap, steering you towards success in the vast and ever-expanding landscape of artificial intelligence.

So, fellow adventurers, as you embark on your AI journey, remember to set your sights on a clear and compelling objective. For in the words of Antoine de Saint-Exupéry, "A goal without a plan is just a wish." Let your objective be your guiding star, lighting the way to a future where AI serves humanity with purpose and clarity.

Safe travels, and may your objectives be as bold as your aspirations.

—-

This captivating teaching emphasizes the importance of defining a clear objective in AI development, using vivid imagery and metaphors to engage and inspire the audience.

7. Collaboration and Communication:

Defining the objective is not a solitary endeavor. It requires collaboration and communication among stakeholders, including domain experts, data scientists, engineers, and end-users. By involving diverse perspectives from the outset, you ensure that the objective aligns with the needs and priorities of all stakeholders, fostering buy-in and support throughout the project lifecycle.

8. Iterative Refinement:

The process of defining the objective is not a one-time event but rather an iterative journey of refinement and clarification. As you gain new insights, feedback, and data, be prepared to revisit and adjust your objective to ensure its relevance and alignment with evolving needs and circumstances.

9. Inspiring Vision:

A well-crafted objective is more than just a destination; it's a vision that inspires and motivates everyone involved in the AI project. It articulates the purpose and significance of the endeavor, instilling a sense of purpose and passion that fuels innovation and perseverance in the face of challenges.

10. Continuous Learning:

Finally, embrace the journey of defining the objective as an opportunity for continuous learning and growth. Each AI project presents unique challenges and opportunities, providing valuable lessons and insights that inform future endeavors. By approaching the process with curiosity, humility, and a willingness to learn, you not only enhance the success of your current project but also lay the foundation for future breakthroughs and discoveries in the dynamic field of artificial intelligence.

In summary, defining the objective is more than just a practical necessity; it's a transformative journey that shapes the trajectory and impact of AI projects. By embracing clarity, collaboration, adaptability, and vision, you set the stage for success, innovation, and ethical leadership in the exciting frontier of artificial intelligence.

So, fellow travelers on the AI journey, let us embark together with clarity of purpose, courage of conviction, and a steadfast commitment to excellence. For in the quest to define the objective lies the promise of a future where AI serves as a force for good, enriching lives, empowering communities, and advancing humanity towards ever greater heights of knowledge, creativity, and compassion.

Bon voyage, and may your objectives be as bold as your dreams!

—-

This continuation reinforces the importance of collaboration, iteration, inspiration, and continuous learning in the process of defining objectives in AI development, encouraging the audience to approach the journey with openness, curiosity, and determination.

11. Alignment with Organizational Goals:

When defining the objective for an AI project, it's crucial to ensure alignment with broader organizational goals and strategies. By anchoring the objective within the context of organizational priorities, you not only increase the project's chances of success but also demonstrate its value in driving tangible business outcomes.

12. Risk Assessment and Mitigation:

As you define the objective, consider potential risks and challenges that may arise along the way. Conduct a thorough risk assessment and develop strategies to mitigate these risks, ensuring that the project remains on track and resilient in the face of adversity.

13. User-Centric Design:

Put the end-user at the center of the objective-setting process. Consider their needs, preferences, and pain points to ensure that the AI solution ultimately delivers value and enhances user experience. By prioritizing user-centric design, you foster adoption and engagement, driving the success and sustainability of the project.

14. Long-Term Vision:

While the immediate objective provides focus and direction, it's essential to also consider the long-term vision for the AI project. Where do you envision the project evolving in the months and years to come? By articulating a compelling long-term vision, you inspire continuity, investment, and innovation, laying the groundwork for sustained impact and growth.

15. Flexibility and Adaptation:

In the dynamic landscape of AI development, flexibility and adaptation are paramount. As you define the objective, remain open to new opportunities, emerging technologies, and evolving market trends. Be prepared to pivot and adjust course as needed, leveraging insights and feedback to optimize outcomes and seize new opportunities for advancement.

16. Celebrate Milestones:

Along the AI journey, take time to celebrate milestones and achievements, no matter how small. Recognize and acknowledge the hard work, creativity, and perseverance of everyone involved in the project. Celebrating milestones not only boosts morale and motivation but also fosters a culture of appreciation and collaboration, fueling continued success and momentum.

17. Reflect and Learn:

Finally, as you reach the culmination of your AI project, take time to reflect on the journey and extract key lessons learned. What worked well? What could be improved? By engaging in thoughtful reflection and learning, you not only enhance your own skills and expertise but also contribute valuable insights to the broader AI community, advancing the collective pursuit of knowledge and innovation.

In conclusion, the process of defining the objective in AI development is not merely a procedural step but a transformative journey that shapes the trajectory and impact of the project. By embracing alignment, risk mitigation, user-centric design, long-term vision, flexibility, celebration, and reflection, you pave the way for success, resilience, and growth in the dynamic and exhilarating field of artificial intelligence.

So, fellow pioneers of AI, let us embark on this journey with clarity of purpose, resilience of spirit, and a shared commitment to excellence. For in the quest to define the objective lies the promise of a future where AI serves as a catalyst for positive change, empowering individuals, organizations, and societies to thrive in an ever-evolving world of possibilities.

Onward, with courage and conviction, towards a future where AI enriches lives, expands horizons, and unlocks the boundless potential of human ingenuity and imagination.

—-

This continuation emphasizes the importance of alignment, risk mitigation, user-centric design, long-term vision, flexibility, celebration, reflection, and continuous learning in the process of defining objectives in AI development, encouraging the audience to approach the journey with resilience, collaboration, and a commitment to excellence.

2

Data Collection

2. Data Collection: Navigating the Sea of Information

Welcome aboard our AI journey, where we now set sail into the vast sea of data collection. Just as a skilled navigator charts a course through treacherous waters, so too must we carefully collect and curate the data that will fuel our AI endeavors.

1. Identify Relevant Data Sources:

The first step in data collection is to identify and gather relevant sources of information. This may include structured data from databases, unstructured data from text documents, images, videos, or even real-time streaming data from sensors and IoT devices. Cast your nets wide, for the richness of your data will determine the depth of your insights.

2. Quality over Quantity:

While it's tempting to amass as much data as possible, quality should always take precedence over quantity. Ensure that your data is accurate, reliable, and representative of the problem you're seeking to solve. Conduct thorough data validation and cleansing to remove errors, outliers, and biases that could skew your results.

3. Ethical Considerations:

As stewards of data, we bear a solemn responsibility to uphold ethical principles and safeguard the privacy and dignity of individuals. Be mindful of consent, transparency, and fairness in your data collection practices, and always prioritize the protection of sensitive information.

4. Data Governance and Compliance:

Adhere to legal and regulatory requirements governing data collection, storage, and usage. Establish robust data governance policies and procedures to ensure compliance with laws such as GDPR, HIPAA, or industry-specific regulations. By building trust and accountability into your data practices, you foster confidence and credibility in your AI initiatives.

5. Data Augmentation and Enrichment:

Sometimes, the data you need may not exist in its ideal form. In such cases, employ techniques like data augmentation and enrichment to enhance the quantity and quality of your dataset. This could involve generating synthetic data, combining multiple sources, or enriching existing data with additional features or metadata.

6. Continuous Iteration and Improvement:

Data collection is not a one-time event but an ongoing process of iteration and improvement. As your AI project evolves, continue to collect feedback, monitor performance, and refine your data collection strategy accordingly. Embrace a mindset of continuous learning and adaptation to ensure that your data remains relevant and effective in driving meaningful insights and outcomes.

7. Collaboration and Partnerships:

Forge partnerships and collaborations with domain experts, data providers, and other stakeholders to access specialized knowledge and resources. By tapping into external expertise and networks, you can expand the breadth and depth of your data collection efforts, enriching your dataset and uncovering new opportunities for innovation and discovery.

8. Empowerment through Data Literacy:

Finally, empower individuals within your organization with the knowledge and skills to navigate the complexities of data collection. Invest in data literacy training and education to cultivate a culture of data-driven decision-making and innovation, where everyone plays a role in harnessing the power of data to drive positive change.

In conclusion, data collection is the cornerstone of AI development, laying the foundation for informed decision-making, predictive analytics, and intelligent automation. By approaching data collection with diligence, integrity, and foresight, we unlock the potential of data to fuel innovation, empower individuals, and transform industries for the betterment of society.

So, fellow voyagers on the AI journey, let us navigate the seas of data with purpose and precision, guided by the principles of quality, ethics, collaboration, and continuous improvement. For in the depths of our data lies the promise of discovery, insight, and impact beyond imagination.

Fair winds and following seas, as we chart a course towards a future where AI enhances lives, enriches communities, and illuminates the path to a brighter tomorrow.

—-

This continuation delves into the intricacies of data collection in AI development, highlighting the importance of quality, ethics, governance, augmentation, collaboration, and empowerment in navigating the sea of information.

9. Data Security and Privacy:

In our quest for valuable data, we must also prioritize the security and privacy of sensitive information. Implement robust security measures to protect data against unauthorized access, breaches, and cyber threats. Adhere to privacy regulations such as GDPR and CCPA, ensuring that data collection practices respect individual rights and preferences. By safeguarding data integrity and confidentiality, we uphold trust and confidence in our AI initiatives.

10. Diversity and Representation:

Ensure diversity and representation in your data collection efforts to avoid biases and ensure fairness in AI algorithms. Be mindful of demographic, cultural, and socioeconomic factors that may influence the data and its interpretation. Actively seek out diverse perspectives and voices to enrich your dataset and promote inclusivity and equity in AI applications.

11. Data Documentation and Metadata:

Document your data collection process thoroughly, including metadata that provides context and insights into the characteristics and origin of the data. Maintain clear records of data sources, collection methods, preprocessing steps, and any transformations applied to the data. By documenting your data pipeline effectively, you facilitate transparency, reproducibility, and accountability in AI development.

12. Data Storage and Management:

Establish robust data storage and management practices to ensure accessibility, scalability, and reliability of your data assets. Utilize secure and scalable storage solutions, such as cloud-based platforms or on-premises data warehouses, that support the diverse needs of your AI projects. Implement data lifecycle management strategies to effectively manage data retention, archival, and deletion in accordance with regulatory requirements and organizational policies.

13. Data Integration and Interoperability:

Integrate disparate data sources and systems to create a unified and interoperable data ecosystem. Break down silos and enable seamless data exchange and collaboration across departments, teams, and external partners. Invest in data integration tools and technologies that facilitate data harmonization, transformation, and synchronization, empowering your organization to leverage the full potential of its data assets.

14. Feedback Loops and Iterative Learning:

Establish feedback loops and mechanisms for iterative learning and improvement based on insights gained from data collection and analysis. Solicit feedback from end-users, stakeholders, and AI models themselves to identify opportunities for optimization and refinement. Embrace a culture of experimentation and adaptation, where feedback drives continuous iteration and enhancement of data collection strategies and AI models.

15. Future-Proofing and Scalability:

Anticipate future needs and scalability requirements when designing your data collection infrastructure and processes. Plan for growth and expansion by adopting scalable architectures, technologies, and methodologies that can accommodate increasing volumes of data and evolving business demands. Embrace agile and modular approaches to data collection that enable flexibility, agility, and responsiveness to changing requirements and opportunities.

In summary, data collection is a multifaceted endeavor that requires careful attention to security, privacy, diversity, documentation, storage, integration, feedback, and scalability. By embracing best practices and principles in data collection, we harness the transformative power of data to drive innovation, insight, and impact in the dynamic and ever-evolving landscape of artificial intelligence.

So, fellow navigators of the data seas, let us chart a course towards a future where data collection serves as a catalyst for positive change, empowerment, and enlightenment. For in the depths of our data lies the potential to unlock new horizons and possibilities beyond imagination.

Smooth sailing, as we navigate the currents of data towards a brighter tomorrow.

—-

This continuation delves deeper into the intricacies of data collection, exploring themes such as security, privacy, diversity, documentation, storage, integration, feedback, scalability, and future-proofing.

16. Collaboration with Data Providers:

Forge partnerships and collaborations with data providers, both within and outside your organization, to access diverse and high-quality data sources. Engage with data vendors, research institutions, government agencies, and open data initiatives to augment your dataset with valuable insights and perspectives. By leveraging external expertise and resources, you enrich your data collection efforts and unlock new opportunities for innovation and discovery.

17. Automation and Streamlining:

Explore automation tools and technologies to streamline the data collection process and improve efficiency. Implement data collection pipelines, workflows, and scripts that automate repetitive tasks such as data extraction, transformation, and loading (ETL). Leverage AI-driven solutions such as web scrapers, data crawlers, and natural language processing (NLP) algorithms to extract and process data from diverse sources with minimal manual intervention.

18. Data Validation and Quality Assurance:

Prioritize data validation and quality assurance to ensure the accuracy, completeness, and reliability of your dataset. Implement rigorous validation checks, data profiling techniques, and outlier detection algorithms to identify and rectify errors, inconsistencies, and anomalies in the data. Conduct thorough data audits and quality assessments to maintain the integrity and trustworthiness of your data assets throughout the data lifecycle.

19. Data Privacy-Preserving Techniques:

Deploy privacy-preserving techniques and technologies to protect sensitive information while still extracting valuable insights from the data. Explore methods such as differential privacy, federated learning, and homomorphic encryption to enable secure and privacy-preserving data analysis and model training. By safeguarding privacy rights and preserving confidentiality, you foster trust and confidence in your AI initiatives among users and stakeholders.

20. Continuous Monitoring and Governance:

Establish robust monitoring and governance mechanisms to track data quality, usage, and compliance over time. Implement data monitoring tools and dashboards that provide real-time visibility into data health, performance, and security metrics. Enforce data governance policies, access controls, and audit trails to ensure accountability, traceability, and compliance with regulatory requirements and organizational standards.

21. Data Ethics and Responsible AI:

Integrate ethical considerations and principles into your data collection practices to promote responsible and ethical AI development. Embrace principles such as fairness, transparency, accountability, and bias mitigation throughout the data lifecycle. Implement mechanisms for informed consent, data anonymization, and algorithmic fairness to uphold ethical standards and societal values in AI applications.

22. Community Engagement and Collaboration:

Engage with the broader AI and data science community to share knowledge, best practices, and lessons learned in data collection. Participate in forums, conferences, and online communities to exchange ideas, collaborate on projects, and contribute to advancing the field of data science. By fostering a culture of collaboration and knowledge sharing, you enrich your own understanding and contribute to the collective growth and advancement of the AI community.

In conclusion, data collection is a multifaceted endeavor that requires collaboration, automation, validation, privacy preservation, monitoring, governance, ethics, and community engagement. By embracing best practices and principles in data collection, we unlock the transformative power of data to drive innovation, insight, and impact in AI development and beyond.

So, fellow stewards of data, let us navigate the complexities of data collection with integrity, diligence, and foresight. For in the depths of our data lies the potential to illuminate the path to a future where AI serves humanity with wisdom, compassion, and empowerment.

Fair winds and following seas, as we chart a course towards a brighter tomorrow.

—

This continuation delves even further into advanced aspects of data collection, exploring themes such as collaboration with data providers, automation, data validation, privacy-preserving techniques, continuous monitoring and governance, data ethics, responsible AI, and community engagement.

3

Data Processing

3. Data Preprocessing: Refining the Raw Material

Ahoy, adventurers! As we continue our voyage through the realms of artificial intelligence, we now embark on the crucial phase of data preprocessing. Just as a skilled craftsman refines raw materials into works of art, so too must we preprocess our data to prepare it for the transformative alchemy of AI.

1. Cleaning and Handling Missing Values:

Our first task is to clean the data, removing any impurities and inconsistencies that may obscure its true essence. Identify and handle missing values, outliers, and errors using techniques such as imputation, interpolation, or deletion. By ensuring data cleanliness, we lay the foundation for accurate and reliable analysis.

2. Feature Engineering and Selection:

Next, we sculpt our data into a more refined form through feature engineering and selection. Extract meaningful features from raw data that capture relevant patterns and relationships. Use domain knowledge, statistical techniques, and machine learning algorithms to identify and select the most informative features for our AI models. By focusing on quality over quantity, we enhance the predictive power and interpretability of our models.

3. Normalization and Scaling:

With our features in hand, we now normalize and scale the data to ensure uniformity and comparability across different features and scales. Apply techniques such as min-max scaling, standardization, or robust scaling to transform the data into a standardized range. By normalizing the data, we mitigate the influence of varying scales and magnitudes, improving the convergence and performance of our AI models.

4. Dimensionality Reduction:

In the vast expanse of data, complexity often lurks in the shadows. To tame this complexity, we employ dimensionality reduction techniques to distill the essence of our data into a more manageable form. Explore methods such as principal component analysis (PCA), t-distributed stochastic neighbor embedding (t-SNE), or feature selection algorithms to reduce the dimensionality of our dataset while preserving its essential structure and information.

5. Handling Categorical Data:

Ah, the diverse tapestry of categorical data! To integrate these categorical variables into our analysis, we encode them into a numerical format that our AI models can understand. Utilize techniques such as one-hot encoding, label encoding, or target encoding to represent categorical variables as numerical features. By bridging the gap between categorical and numerical worlds, we unlock the full potential of our data for analysis and modeling.

6. Text Preprocessing:

Ahoy, mateys! As we navigate the seas of text data, we encounter a treasure trove of linguistic riches waiting to be unearthed. But first, we must preprocess this textual bounty to extract its hidden gems. Cleanse the text by removing stopwords, punctuation, and special characters. Tokenize the text into words or n-grams, and apply techniques such as stemming or lemmatization to reduce words to their root forms. By preprocessing text data effectively, we uncover its underlying structure and semantics, enabling powerful analysis and insight.

7. Image Preprocessing:

Behold, the canvas of the digital age! As we embark on our journey through image data, we must prepare these visual masterpieces for analysis and interpretation. Normalize the pixel values to a standardized range, and apply techniques such as resizing, cropping, or augmentation to enhance the quality and diversity of our image dataset. By preprocessing image data with care and precision, we unlock its expressive potential and reveal insights hidden within the pixels.

8. Temporal Preprocessing:

Ah, the passage of time, a river flowing through the landscape of data. To capture the dynamics of temporal data, we preprocess time series and sequential data with finesse. Extract meaningful features such as trends, seasonality, and periodicity using techniques such as differencing, smoothing, or Fourier analysis. By preprocessing temporal data effectively, we uncover patterns and trends that illuminate the past and forecast the future.

In conclusion, data preprocessing is a vital step in the journey from raw data to actionable insights in artificial intelligence. By cleaning, transforming, and refining our data with care and precision, we prepare it for the transformative alchemy of AI, unlocking its hidden potential and revealing insights that propel us towards our goals.

So, fellow adventurers, let us embark on this voyage of data preprocessing with diligence, creativity, and a spirit of discovery. For in the depths of our data lies the key to unlocking the mysteries of the universe and shaping the future of artificial intelligence.

Fair winds and clear skies, as we navigate the seas of data towards new horizons and discoveries.

This continuation delves into the essential aspects of data preprocessing, exploring themes such as cleaning, feature engineering, normalization, scaling, dimensionality reduction, handling categorical data, text preprocessing, image preprocessing, and temporal preprocessing.

9. Handling Imbalanced Data:

In the vast ocean of data, we sometimes encounter imbalances where certain classes or categories are disproportionately represented. To navigate these turbulent waters, we employ techniques to address imbalanced data. Explore methods such as resampling (oversampling or undersampling), synthetic data generation, or algorithmic approaches (e.g., cost-sensitive learning or ensemble methods) to rebalance the distribution of classes and improve model performance. By mitigating the impact of imbalanced data, we ensure fairness and robustness in our AI models.

10. Time Series Decomposition:

When faced with time series data, we often encounter complex patterns and trends that obscure underlying structures. To reveal the hidden dynamics of time, we decompose time series data into its constituent components. Apply methods such as trend extraction, seasonal decomposition, and residual analysis to decompose time series into trend, seasonal, and residual components. By decomposing time series effectively, we extract actionable insights and forecast future trends with greater accuracy and reliability.

11. Handling Outliers:

Outliers, like rogue waves in the ocean, can wreak havoc on our data analysis and modeling efforts. To navigate these treacherous waters, we identify and handle outliers with care and precision. Utilize statistical techniques such as Z-score, modified Z-score, or robust methods (e.g., median absolute deviation) to detect outliers based on their deviation from the norm. Consider the nature of the data and domain-specific knowledge to determine whether outliers should be removed, transformed, or treated separately. By addressing outliers effectively, we improve the robustness and validity of our AI models.

12. Data Augmentation:

In the quest for diverse and representative data, we often seek to augment our dataset with synthetic examples that capture variations and nuances. Employ data augmentation techniques such as rotation, translation, scaling, flipping, or adding noise to generate synthetic data samples. These augmented samples enrich our dataset, improving the generalization and robustness of our AI models. By embracing data augmentation, we expand the horizons of our data and unlock new opportunities for learning and discovery.

13. Handling Multimodal Data:

As we navigate the multidimensional landscape of data, we encounter diverse modalities such as text, images, audio, and sensor data. To integrate these multimodal sources effectively, we employ techniques for handling multimodal data. Explore methods such as fusion, concatenation, or attention mechanisms to combine information from different modalities into a unified representation. By harnessing the complementary strengths of multimodal data, we enhance the richness and depth of our analysis and modeling capabilities.

14. Handling Skewed Distributions:

In the distribution of our data, we sometimes encounter skewness where the data is asymmetrically distributed. To address skewed distributions, we apply techniques that transform the data to achieve symmetry and balance. Explore methods such as log transformation, power transformation, or box-cox transformation to normalize the distribution and reduce skewness. By mitigating the effects of skewed distributions, we improve the interpretability and performance of our AI models.

15. Handling Complex Relationships:

In the intricate web of data, we often encounter complex relationships and interactions between variables that defy simple linear models. To capture these complex relationships, we employ techniques that model non-linear and higher-order interactions. Explore methods such as polynomial regression, kernel methods, or tree-based models to capture complex patterns and dependencies in the data. By embracing complexity, we unlock new insights and predictive power in our AI models.

In conclusion, data preprocessing is a nuanced and multifaceted endeavor that requires careful consideration of imbalanced data, time series decomposition, outlier handling, data augmentation, multimodal integration, skewed distributions, and complex relationships. By navigating these challenges with skill and creativity, we refine our data into a form that unleashes the full potential of artificial intelligence to drive innovation, insight, and impact.

So, fellow adventurers, let us continue our voyage through the seas of data preprocessing with courage, ingenuity, and a relentless pursuit of excellence. For in the depths of our data lies the key to unlocking the mysteries of the universe and shaping the destiny of artificial intelligence.

Fair winds and steady sails, as we chart a course towards new horizons and discoveries.

—-

This continuation explores advanced aspects of data preprocessing, including handling imbalanced data, time series decomposition, outlier handling, data augmentation, multimodal integration, skewed distributions, and complex relationships.

16. Data Compression:

In the vast expanse of data, we often encounter high-dimensional spaces that strain our computational resources and limit the efficiency of our algorithms. To navigate these challenges, we employ techniques for data compression. Explore methods such as feature hashing, autoencoders, or dimensionality reduction algorithms like t-Distributed Stochastic Neighbor Embedding (t-SNE) to compress high-dimensional data into a more compact representation. By reducing the dimensionality of our data, we conserve resources, accelerate computation, and facilitate more efficient analysis and modeling.

17. Handling Time Delays and Lags:

When working with time series and sequential data, we must account for time delays and lags that reflect temporal dependencies and dynamics. To capture these temporal relationships, we incorporate lagged features into our dataset. Generate lagged variables by shifting the values of time-dependent variables forward or backward in time. By encoding time delays and lags effectively, we capture temporal patterns and dependencies that enhance the predictive power and interpretability of our models.

18. Addressing Data Drift and Concept Drift:

In the ever-changing landscape of data, we encounter shifts and drifts over time that challenge the stability and performance of our AI models. To address data drift and concept drift, we implement techniques for monitoring and adaptation. Establish monitoring mechanisms to detect changes in the data distribution or underlying concepts. Employ strategies such as model retraining, domain adaptation, or transfer learning to adapt our models to evolving data patterns. By addressing data drift and concept drift proactively, we maintain the relevance and effectiveness of our AI solutions over time.

19. Exploratory Data Analysis (EDA):

Before embarking on the journey of modeling and prediction, we embark on a voyage of exploration through the seas of data. Conduct exploratory data analysis (EDA) to gain insights into the characteristics, patterns, and relationships within our dataset. Visualize the data through histograms, scatter plots, heatmaps, and other graphical techniques to uncover trends, outliers, and correlations. By exploring the data with curiosity and diligence, we lay the groundwork for informed decision-making and hypothesis generation in our AI endeavors.

20. Data Sampling Techniques:

In the realm of large and complex datasets, we often face challenges of scalability and computational burden. To overcome these challenges, we employ data sampling techniques to extract representative subsets of our data for analysis and modeling. Explore methods such as random sampling, stratified sampling, or cluster-based sampling to select samples that preserve the distribution and characteristics of the original dataset. By leveraging data sampling effectively, we accelerate computation, conserve resources, and facilitate more efficient exploration and experimentation with our data.

21. Cross-Validation:

As we traverse the terrain of model development and evaluation, we encounter pitfalls of overfitting and model selection bias. To navigate these challenges, we employ cross-validation techniques to assess the generalization performance of our models. Partition the dataset into multiple subsets (folds), and iteratively train and evaluate the model on different combinations of training and validation data. By cross-validating our models rigorously, we obtain more robust estimates of performance and reduce the risk of overfitting, ensuring the reliability and validity of our AI solutions.

In conclusion, data preprocessing is a dynamic and iterative process that requires creativity, adaptability, and domain expertise. By navigating the challenges of data compression, time delays, data drift, exploratory data analysis, data sampling, and cross-validation, we refine our data into a form that empowers us to unlock insights, make informed decisions, and drive innovation in artificial intelligence.

So, fellow adventurers, let us continue our journey through the seas of data preprocessing with resilience, curiosity, and a commitment to excellence. For in the depths of our data lies the potential to transform our understanding of the world and shape the future of artificial intelligence.

Fair winds and clear skies, as we chart a course towards new horizons and discoveries.

—-

This continuation explores further advanced aspects of data preprocessing, including data compression, handling time delays and lags, addressing data drift and concept drift, exploratory data analysis (EDA), data sampling techniques, and cross-validation.

4

Model Selection and Development

4. Model Selection and Development: Navigating the Path to Intelligence

Ahoy, fellow travelers! As we embark on the next leg of our AI journey, we set our sights on model selection and development, where the magic of artificial intelligence begins to take shape. Just as a skilled navigator selects the right vessel for the journey ahead, so too must we choose the most suitable models to navigate the seas of data and unlock its hidden treasures.

1. Define the Problem and Objectives:

Before setting sail into the realm of modeling, we must first chart our course by defining the problem and objectives of our AI endeavor. Clarify the goals, scope, and success criteria of the project, ensuring alignment with stakeholder needs and organizational priorities. By establishing a clear roadmap, we lay the foundation for informed decision-making and effective model selection.

2. Explore Model Options:

With our objectives in mind, we cast our gaze upon the vast array of modeling techniques and algorithms at our disposal. Explore a variety of model options, ranging from classical statistical methods to modern machine learning and deep learning approaches. Consider the characteristics of the data, complexity of the problem, interpretability requirements, and computational constraints when selecting candidate models. By evaluating multiple options, we identify the most promising candidates for further exploration and development.

3. Understand Model Assumptions and Limitations:

As we delve deeper into the realm of modeling, we must heed the assumptions and limitations of each approach. Understand the underlying assumptions, strengths, and weaknesses of the selected models, and assess their suitability for the specific problem at hand. Consider factors such as linearity, distributional assumptions, feature interactions, and robustness to noisy or missing data. By acknowledging the limitations of our models, we mitigate the risk of misinterpretation and ensure the reliability of our results.

4. Feature Engineering and Selection:

Prepare the data for modeling by refining and selecting relevant features that capture the essential characteristics of the problem. Leverage insights from exploratory data analysis and domain knowledge to engineer informative features that enhance the predictive power of the models. Employ techniques such as dimensionality reduction, feature scaling, and transformation to streamline the feature space and improve model efficiency. By curating a well-crafted feature set, we empower our models to uncover meaningful patterns and relationships within the data.

5. Model Training and Evaluation:

With our data prepared and features selected, we set sail into the waters of model training and evaluation. Split the dataset into training, validation, and test sets, and train the selected models on the training data. Fine-tune model hyperparameters using techniques such as grid search, random search, or Bayesian optimization to optimize performance. Evaluate model performance on the validation set using appropriate metrics such as accuracy, precision, recall, F1-score, or area under the ROC curve (AUC). Iterate on the model development process, refining the models based on feedback from the validation results.

6. Ensemble Methods and Model Stacking:

In the pursuit of superior performance and robustness, we turn to the power of ensemble methods and model stacking. Combine multiple models into an ensemble, leveraging the wisdom of crowds to achieve better predictive performance than any individual model alone. Explore techniques such as bagging, boosting, or stacking to ensemble diverse models and exploit their complementary strengths. By harnessing the collective intelligence of ensemble methods, we enhance the resilience and accuracy of our AI solutions.

7. Interpretability and Explainability:

As we navigate the complex terrain of AI modeling, we must strive for transparency and interpretability in our models. Seek models that not only achieve high predictive performance but also provide insights into the underlying decision-making process. Explore techniques such as feature importance analysis, partial dependence plots, or model-agnostic interpretability methods to understand and explain the behavior of the models. By fostering interpretability and explainability, we build trust and confidence in our AI solutions among users and stakeholders.

8. Model Deployment and Monitoring:

With our models trained and validated, we prepare to deploy them into operational environments where they can make a tangible impact. Implement robust deployment pipelines and monitoring systems to ensure the reliability, scalability, and performance of the deployed models. Continuously monitor model performance and feedback from end-users, and iterate on the models as needed to adapt to changing conditions and evolving requirements. By embracing a culture of continuous improvement and iteration, we maximize the value and effectiveness of our AI solutions in real-world settings.

In conclusion, model selection and development are pivotal stages in the journey from data to intelligence in artificial intelligence. By defining clear objectives, exploring model options, understanding assumptions and limitations, engineering informative features, training and evaluating models, leveraging ensemble methods, ensuring interpretability, and deploying models effectively, we unlock the transformative power of AI to drive innovation, insight, and impact in diverse domains and applications.

So, fellow voyagers on the AI journey, let us navigate the waters of model selection and development with skill, ingenuity, and a spirit of discovery. For in the depths of our models lies the potential to unlock new horizons and illuminate the path to a future where AI serves humanity with wisdom, compassion, and empowerment.

Fair winds and following seas, as we chart a course towards new frontiers and discoveries.

—-

This continuation delves into the essential aspects of model selection and development in AI, exploring themes such as defining objectives, exploring model options, understanding assumptions and limitations, feature engineering and selection, model training and evaluation, ensemble methods, interpretability, and deployment and monitoring.

9. Hyperparameter Tuning:

In the pursuit of optimal model performance, we embark on the quest of hyperparameter tuning. Fine-tune the hyperparameters of our models to maximize their effectiveness and generalization ability. Explore techniques such as grid search, random search, or Bayesian optimization to search the hyperparameter space and identify the configuration that yields the best performance on the validation set. By tuning hyperparameters meticulously, we unlock the full potential of our models and achieve superior predictive accuracy and robustness.

10. Transfer Learning:

In the realm of AI, we often encounter scenarios where data is scarce or domain-specific knowledge is limited. To address these challenges, we turn to the power of transfer learning. Transfer knowledge from pre-trained models on large, general-purpose datasets to tasks with limited data or specific domains. Fine-tune the pre-trained models on our target task or domain, leveraging the knowledge encoded in their learned representations. By harnessing transfer learning, we accelerate model development, improve generalization, and overcome data scarcity and domain-specific challenges.

11. Model Interpretation Techniques:

As we navigate the complexities of AI models, we seek to unravel their inner workings and understand the rationale behind their predictions. Deploy model interpretation techniques to interpret and explain the decisions made by our models. Explore methods such as feature importance analysis, SHAP (SHapley Additive exPlanations), LIME (Local Interpretable Model-agnostic Explanations), or surrogate models to elucidate the factors influencing model predictions and uncover insights into the data. By promoting transparency and interpretability, we build trust and understanding in our AI solutions among users and stakeholders.

12. Model Optimization for Efficiency:

In the era of big data and resource constraints, we strive to optimize our models for efficiency and scalability. Explore techniques for model optimization that reduce computational complexity, memory footprint, and inference latency without sacrificing performance. Employ methods such as model pruning, quantization, compression, or architecture optimization to streamline the size and complexity of our models. By optimizing for efficiency, we enhance the deployability, scalability, and cost-effectiveness of our AI solutions, making them accessible and practical for real-world applications.

13. Model Robustness and Security:

In the face of adversarial attacks and unforeseen challenges, we fortify our models with robustness and security measures. Assess the vulnerability of our models to adversarial examples, data perturbations, or model inversion attacks, and implement defenses to mitigate these risks. Explore techniques such as adversarial training, input sanitization, or robust optimization to enhance the resilience of our models against malicious actors and unforeseen perturbations. By prioritizing robustness and security, we safeguard the integrity and reliability of our AI solutions in the face of adversities and threats.

14. Ethical Considerations and Bias Mitigation:

As guardians of AI, we bear a solemn responsibility to uphold ethical principles and mitigate biases in our models. Assess the ethical implications and potential biases inherent in our data and modeling approaches, and implement strategies to mitigate these biases and ensure fairness and equity in our AI solutions. Explore techniques such as bias detection, fairness-aware learning, or debiasing algorithms to identify and address biases related to sensitive attributes such as race, gender, or socioeconomic status. By promoting fairness and equity, we foster trust, inclusivity, and social responsibility in our AI initiatives, making them beneficial for all members of society.

15. Continuous Learning and Adaptation:

In the dynamic landscape of AI, we embrace a mindset of continuous learning and adaptation to stay abreast of emerging trends, technologies, and challenges. Stay informed about the latest developments in AI research, methodologies, and best practices, and incorporate new insights and techniques into our modeling workflows. Engage in lifelong learning and professional development to expand our skills, expertise, and understanding of AI principles and applications. By embracing continuous learning and adaptation, we remain agile, innovative, and resilient in the face of change, driving progress and excellence in the field of artificial intelligence.

In conclusion, model selection and development in artificial intelligence require a comprehensive approach that encompasses hyperparameter tuning, transfer learning, model interpretation, optimization for efficiency, robustness and security, ethical considerations, bias mitigation, and continuous learning and adaptation. By navigating these challenges with diligence, creativity, and a commitment to excellence, we unlock the transformative power of AI to drive innovation, insight, and impact in diverse domains and applications.

So, fellow adventurers on the AI journey, let us continue our quest for intelligence with courage, curiosity, and a spirit of exploration. For in the depths of our models lies the potential to unlock new frontiers and shape the future of artificial intelligence for the betterment of humanity.

Fair winds and clear skies, as we chart a course towards new horizons and discoveries.

——-

This continuation explores advanced aspects of model selection and development in AI, including hyperparameter tuning, transfer learning, model interpretation techniques, model optimization for efficiency, model robustness and security, ethical considerations and bias mitigation, and continuous learning and adaptation.

16. Model Deployment Strategies:

Upon crafting our AI models, we face the pivotal challenge of deploying them into operational environments where they can make a tangible impact. Explore various deployment strategies to seamlessly integrate our models into production systems. Consider options such as cloud-based deployment, edge computing, containerization, or serverless architectures, depending on the specific requirements and constraints of the deployment environment. By adopting efficient deployment strategies, we ensure the scalability, reliability, and accessibility of our AI solutions, enabling them to deliver value to end-users and stakeholders.

17. Monitoring and Performance Evaluation:

As our models venture into the wild, we must monitor their performance and behavior in real-world settings to ensure they continue to meet the desired objectives and standards. Implement monitoring systems that track key performance metrics, model drift, and user feedback, providing insights into model performance and behavior over time. Establish protocols for proactive intervention and model retraining based on predefined thresholds or anomalous patterns detected during monitoring. By continuously evaluating and optimizing model performance, we maintain the relevance, reliability, and effectiveness of our AI solutions in dynamic and evolving environments.

18. Feedback Loops and Iterative Improvement:

In the ever-changing landscape of AI, we recognize the importance of feedback loops and iterative improvement in refining our models and algorithms over time. Solicit feedback from end-users, stakeholders, and domain experts to identify areas for enhancement and optimization in our AI solutions. Leverage insights from user interactions, user-generated data, and real-world feedback to iteratively update and iterate on our models, incorporating new features, addressing performance issues, and adapting to changing user needs and preferences. By embracing a culture of continuous improvement and iteration, we foster innovation, agility, and resilience in our AI initiatives, ensuring they remain relevant and impactful in a rapidly evolving world.

19. Collaboration and Knowledge Sharing:

As stewards of AI, we recognize the value of collaboration and knowledge sharing in advancing the field and driving collective progress. Engage with the broader AI community through forums, conferences, and online platforms to share insights, best practices, and lessons learned from our AI projects. Collaborate with peers, researchers, and industry partners on joint initiatives, open-source projects, and collaborative research efforts to tackle common challenges and push the boundaries of AI innovation. By fostering a culture of collaboration and knowledge sharing, we accelerate the pace of discovery, foster creativity, and amplify the impact of our AI endeavors for the benefit of society.

20. Responsible AI Governance and Ethics:

In our pursuit of AI innovation and advancement, we must uphold principles of responsible AI governance and ethics to ensure our AI solutions are developed and deployed in a manner that promotes fairness, transparency, accountability, and societal well-being. Establish governance frameworks, policies, and guidelines that govern the development, deployment, and use of AI technologies within our organizations and communities. Embed ethical considerations, bias mitigation strategies, and human-centric design principles into our AI development processes to safeguard against unintended consequences and promote ethical AI outcomes. By prioritizing responsible AI governance and ethics, we foster trust, inclusivity, and social responsibility in our AI initiatives, making them beneficial for all members of society.

21. Lifelong Learning and Skill Development:

As lifelong learners and practitioners of AI, we recognize the importance of continuous skill development and professional growth to stay abreast of emerging trends, technologies, and methodologies in the field. Invest in ongoing training, education, and professional development opportunities to expand our knowledge, expertise, and proficiency in AI principles, algorithms, and tools. Embrace interdisciplinary learning and cross-functional collaboration to gain insights from diverse perspectives and domains, enriching our understanding and capabilities in AI innovation and application. By cultivating a culture of lifelong learning and skill development, we empower ourselves and our teams to tackle complex challenges, drive innovation, and shape the future of artificial intelligence.

In conclusion, the journey of AI extends far beyond the development of individual models or algorithms; it encompasses a broad spectrum of activities and considerations that span the entire lifecycle of AI innovation and deployment. By embracing strategies for model deployment, monitoring, feedback loops, collaboration, responsible AI governance, and lifelong learning, we navigate the complexities of AI with wisdom, foresight, and a commitment to excellence. Together, let us chart a course towards a future where AI serves humanity with wisdom, compassion, and empowerment, unlocking new horizons and shaping a brighter tomorrow for all.

Fair winds and steady sails, as we embark on this journey of discovery and transformation.

—-

This continuation provides insights into advanced aspects of AI deployment, monitoring, feedback loops, collaboration, responsible AI governance, and lifelong learning.

5

Evaluation and Performance Metrics

5. Evaluation and Performance Metrics:

As we navigate the seas of artificial intelligence, it's imperative to steer our course by reliable metrics that gauge the effectiveness and performance of our models. Explore a range of evaluation metrics tailored to the specific objectives and characteristics of our AI applications. Consider metrics such as accuracy, precision, recall, F1-score, area under the receiver operating characteristic curve (AUC-ROC), mean squared error (MSE), or mean absolute error (MAE), depending on the nature of the task (classification, regression, etc.) and the desired outcome. By selecting appropriate evaluation metrics, we gain insights into the strengths and limitations of our models, enabling informed decision-making and continuous improvement.

6. Cross-Validation and Robustness Testing:

In the quest for reliable and robust AI solutions, we employ techniques such as cross-validation and robustness testing to assess the generalization performance and stability of our models across diverse datasets and conditions. Implement k-fold cross-validation, stratified cross-validation, or leave-one-out cross-validation to evaluate the performance of our models on multiple subsets of the data and mitigate the risk of overfitting. Conduct robustness testing by introducing perturbations, variations, or adversarial examples to the input data and evaluating the model's resilience and performance under different conditions. By validating our models rigorously, we ensure their reliability, generalization ability, and suitability for real-world deployment.

7. Model Explainability and Interpretability:

As custodians of AI, we prioritize transparency and interpretability in our models to foster trust, understanding, and accountability among users and stakeholders. Employ techniques for model explainability and interpretability that elucidate the rationale behind model predictions and decisions. Explore methods such as feature importance analysis, partial dependence plots, local interpretable model-agnostic explanations (LIME), or SHapley Additive exPlanations (SHAP) to uncover insights into the factors influencing model predictions and reveal potential biases or errors in the data. By promoting model explainability and interpretability, we empower users to make informed decisions and foster trust in our AI solutions.

8. Bias Detection and Mitigation:

In our pursuit of ethical and fair AI, we vigilantly detect and mitigate biases that may arise in our data, models, or algorithms, leading to inequitable outcomes or discriminatory practices. Implement techniques for bias detection and mitigation throughout the AI lifecycle, from data collection and preprocessing to model training and evaluation. Conduct bias audits, fairness assessments, and demographic parity analyses to identify disparities and biases related to sensitive attributes such as race, gender, age, or socioeconomic status. Employ strategies such as dataset stratification, fairness-aware learning, or adversarial debiasing to mitigate biases and promote fairness and equity in our AI solutions. By addressing biases proactively, we uphold ethical standards and ensure our AI applications benefit all members of society equitably.

9. Robustness to Adversarial Attacks:

In the age of cybersecurity threats and adversarial manipulation, we fortify our AI solutions with robustness measures to withstand attacks and preserve their integrity and reliability. Assess the vulnerability of our models to adversarial examples, data perturbations, or evasion attacks, and implement defenses to mitigate these risks. Explore techniques such as adversarial training, input sanitization, or model verification to enhance the resilience of our models against malicious actors and unforeseen perturbations. By prioritizing robustness to adversarial attacks, we safeguard the trustworthiness and security of our AI solutions in the face of potential threats.

10. Regulatory Compliance and Ethical Considerations:

In our journey through the realms of AI, we navigate the complex terrain of regulatory compliance and ethical considerations to ensure our AI solutions adhere to legal and ethical standards and respect the rights and dignity of individuals. Stay informed about relevant laws, regulations, and guidelines governing AI development, deployment, and use in various jurisdictions and industries. Embed ethical principles such as transparency, fairness, accountability, and privacy preservation into our AI development processes and decision-making frameworks. Implement measures for informed consent, data anonymization, and algorithmic transparency to protect user privacy and mitigate potential risks and harms associated with AI applications. By prioritizing regulatory compliance and ethical considerations, we uphold societal values and foster trust, integrity, and responsible innovation in our AI initiatives.

11. Continuous Monitoring and Improvement:

In the dynamic landscape of AI, we embrace a culture of continuous monitoring and improvement to ensure the effectiveness, reliability, and relevance of our AI solutions over time. Establish monitoring systems that track key performance metrics, model drift, and user feedback, providing insights into model performance and behavior in real-world settings. Implement mechanisms for proactive intervention and model retraining based on predefined thresholds or anomalous patterns detected during monitoring. Iterate on our AI solutions iteratively, incorporating new data, insights, and feedback to adapt to changing conditions and evolving requirements. By embracing continuous monitoring and improvement, we maximize the value and impact of our AI initiatives, driving innovation and excellence in the field of artificial intelligence.

In conclusion, the evaluation and validation of AI solutions are essential stages in the journey from development to deployment, ensuring the reliability, effectiveness, and ethical integrity of our models and algorithms. By employing robust evaluation metrics, cross-validation techniques, model explainability and interpretability, bias detection and mitigation strategies, robustness to adversarial attacks, regulatory compliance, and continuous monitoring and improvement, we navigate the complexities of AI with diligence, responsibility, and a commitment to excellence. Together, let us chart a course towards a future where AI serves humanity with wisdom, fairness, and empowerment, unlocking new possibilities and shaping a brighter tomorrow for all.

Fair winds and clear skies, as we embark on this journey of discovery and transformation.

—-

This continuation provides insights into essential aspects of evaluating and validating AI solutions, including metrics, cross-validation, model explainability, bias detection and mitigation, robustness to adversarial attacks, regulatory compliance, and continuous monitoring and improvement.

12. Scalability and Performance Optimization:

In the realm of artificial intelligence, scalability and performance optimization are critical considerations to ensure our solutions can handle large-scale data processing and deliver real-time responses with efficiency and reliability. Explore techniques for optimizing the scalability and performance of our AI systems, such as parallel processing, distributed computing, caching mechanisms, and hardware acceleration (e.g., GPUs, TPUs). Design our algorithms and architectures with scalability in mind, employing scalable data structures, algorithms, and frameworks that can efficiently process vast amounts of data in parallel. By optimizing for scalability and performance, we enable our AI solutions to scale seamlessly with growing data volumes and user demands, delivering responsive and efficient experiences to users and stakeholders.

13. Interoperability and Integration:

In the interconnected landscape of modern technology, interoperability and integration are essential for enabling seamless communication and collaboration between diverse systems, platforms, and applications. Design our AI solutions with interoperability in mind, ensuring they can integrate seamlessly with existing infrastructure, data sources, and software ecosystems. Employ standard protocols, APIs, and data formats to facilitate interoperability and enable seamless data exchange and communication between different components and systems. By fostering interoperability and integration, we unlock synergies and opportunities for collaboration, innovation, and value creation across diverse domains and technologies.

14. Human-Centric Design and User Experience:

In our quest to harness the power of artificial intelligence, we must never lose sight of the human element and the importance of designing solutions that prioritize the needs, preferences, and experiences of users. Adopt a human-centric design approach that places users at the center of the design process, empathizing with their goals, challenges, and aspirations. Incorporate user feedback, usability testing, and iterative design cycles to create intuitive, accessible, and engaging user experiences that empower users and enhance their productivity, satisfaction, and well-being. By embracing human-centric design principles, we create AI solutions that are not only technologically advanced but also socially responsible, ethical, and impactful, enriching the lives of users and fostering positive human-AI interactions.

15. Ethical Considerations and Responsible AI:

As stewards of artificial intelligence, we bear a solemn responsibility to ensure our AI solutions are developed and deployed in a manner that upholds ethical principles, respects human rights, and promotes societal well-being. Consider the ethical implications and potential societal impacts of our AI applications, including issues related to privacy, fairness, transparency, accountability, bias, and discrimination. Implement measures to mitigate ethical risks and promote responsible AI, such as ethical impact assessments, fairness-aware algorithms, bias detection and mitigation techniques, and transparency mechanisms. By prioritizing ethical considerations and responsible AI practices, we build trust, foster inclusivity, and uphold the values of integrity, fairness, and respect in our AI initiatives, making them beneficial for all members of society.

16. Regulatory Compliance and Legal Frameworks:

In the complex regulatory landscape of artificial intelligence, we must navigate a maze of laws, regulations, and legal frameworks governing the development, deployment, and use of AI technologies. Stay informed about relevant regulatory requirements and legal obligations applicable to our AI applications, including data protection, privacy, intellectual property, cybersecurity, and consumer protection laws. Ensure our AI solutions comply with applicable regulations and standards, and establish governance frameworks and risk management practices to mitigate legal and compliance risks. By prioritizing regulatory compliance and adherence to legal frameworks, we uphold legal standards, mitigate legal risks, and build trust and confidence among users, stakeholders, and regulators in our AI initiatives.

17. Societal Impact and Ethical Use Cases:

As creators and users of artificial intelligence, we have a duty to consider the broader societal impact and ethical implications of our AI applications, ensuring they contribute positively to the well-being and advancement of society. Evaluate the potential societal benefits and risks associated with our AI solutions, including their impact on employment, education, healthcare, transportation, environment, and social equity. Prioritize ethical use cases and applications that align with societal values, address pressing societal challenges, and promote positive social outcomes, such as improving healthcare access, enhancing education opportunities, advancing environmental sustainability, and fostering inclusive economic growth. By championing ethical use cases and societal impact initiatives, we harness the transformative power of AI to create a better, more equitable, and sustainable future for all members of society.

18. Transparency and Accountability:

In our journey through the realms of artificial intelligence, we must uphold principles of transparency and accountability to ensure our AI solutions are transparent, accountable, and trustworthy. Foster transparency in our AI development processes, algorithms, and decision-making mechanisms, providing users and stakeholders with visibility into how our AI systems work and how decisions are made. Establish mechanisms for accountability and oversight, including clear lines of responsibility, recourse mechanisms, and redress procedures in case of errors, biases, or unintended consequences. By promoting transparency and accountability, we build trust, foster confidence, and mitigate risks associated with AI technologies, empowering users and stakeholders to engage with AI solutions with confidence and trust.

19. Collaboration and Partnerships:

In the collaborative landscape of artificial intelligence, we recognize the importance of collaboration and partnerships in driving innovation, sharing knowledge, and addressing common challenges and opportunities. Foster collaborative partnerships with industry peers, academic institutions, research organizations, startups, and government agencies to leverage complementary expertise, resources, and capabilities in AI research, development, and deployment. Engage in collaborative initiatives, consortia, and open-source projects that promote knowledge sharing, best practices, and standards development in AI technologies and applications. By fostering a culture of collaboration and partnerships, we accelerate the pace of AI innovation, expand the reach and impact of our AI initiatives, and unlock new opportunities for growth and advancement in the field.

20. Lifelong Learning and Professional Development:

As lifelong learners and practitioners of artificial intelligence, we recognize the importance of continuous learning and professional development in staying abreast of emerging trends, technologies, and methodologies in the field. Invest in ongoing training, education, and skill development to expand our knowledge, expertise, and proficiency in AI principles, algorithms, and applications. Embrace interdisciplinary learning and cross-functional collaboration to gain insights from diverse perspectives and domains, enriching our understanding and capabilities in AI innovation and application. By cultivating a culture of lifelong learning and professional development, we empower ourselves and our teams to tackle complex challenges, drive innovation, and shape the future of artificial intelligence.

In conclusion, the ethical and societal dimensions of artificial intelligence are essential considerations that must underpin all aspects of AI research, development, deployment, and use. By embracing ethical principles, prioritizing societal impact, fostering transparency and accountability, ensuring regulatory compliance, promoting collaboration and partnerships, and investing in lifelong learning and professional development, we navigate the complexities of AI with wisdom, responsibility, and a commitment to excellence. Together, let us chart a course towards a future where AI serves humanity with wisdom, compassion, and empowerment, unlocking new possibilities and shaping a brighter tomorrow for all.

Fair winds and steady sails, as we embark on this journey of discovery and transformation.

——-

This continuation dives into the ethical and societal dimensions of artificial intelligence, exploring themes such as human-centric design, responsible AI, regulatory compliance, societal impact, transparency, collaboration, and lifelong learning.

21. Diversity, Equity, and Inclusion in AI:

In our pursuit of artificial intelligence, we recognize the importance of fostering diversity, equity, and inclusion (DEI) within the AI community to promote innovation, creativity, and fairness. Embrace diversity in all its forms, including diversity of backgrounds, perspectives, and experiences, within our AI teams and organizations. Prioritize equity and inclusivity in our hiring practices, career development programs, and organizational policies to ensure equal opportunities and representation for individuals from underrepresented groups in AI, including women, minorities, LGBTQ+ individuals, and individuals with disabilities. By fostering a culture of diversity, equity, and inclusion, we enrich our AI community, unlock untapped talent and potential, and drive greater innovation and impact in the field of artificial intelligence.

22. Global Collaboration and International Cooperation:

In the interconnected world of artificial intelligence, we recognize the importance of global collaboration and international cooperation in addressing shared challenges, advancing knowledge, and harnessing the transformative power of AI for the benefit of all humanity. Foster collaboration and partnerships across borders, cultures, and regions to leverage diverse perspectives, expertise, and resources in AI research, development, and deployment. Engage in international initiatives, consortia, and partnerships that promote knowledge sharing, capacity building, and ethical standards development in AI technologies and applications. By embracing global collaboration and cooperation, we amplify the impact of our AI initiatives, foster mutual understanding and respect, and pave the way for a more inclusive, equitable, and sustainable future for all.

23. Accessibility and AI for All:

In our journey through the realms of artificial intelligence, we strive to ensure that AI technologies and applications are accessible and inclusive, enabling participation and empowerment for all members of society, regardless of age, gender, ability, or socioeconomic status. Design AI solutions with accessibility in mind, incorporating features such as voice interfaces, screen readers, and alternative input methods to accommodate users with disabilities or impairments. Prioritize inclusive design practices that consider diverse user needs and preferences, ensuring our AI solutions are usable and beneficial for individuals with varying levels of technological proficiency and digital literacy. By promoting accessibility and inclusivity, we democratize access to AI technologies and empower individuals to participate fully in the digital age, unlocking new opportunities for learning, creativity, and social connection.

24. Ethical Use of AI in Governance and Decision-Making:

As custodians of artificial intelligence, we bear a solemn responsibility to ensure the ethical use of AI in governance and decision-making processes to uphold democratic values, protect human rights, and promote the public interest. Implement principles of transparency, accountability, and fairness in the design and deployment of AI systems used in governance, public administration, and decision-making contexts. Establish mechanisms for public oversight, citizen engagement, and accountability in AI governance frameworks to ensure that AI technologies are deployed responsibly and ethically, with due consideration for the rights, interests, and welfare of all stakeholders. By promoting ethical use of AI in governance and decision-making, we uphold democratic principles, foster trust in public institutions, and advance the collective well-being of society.

25. AI for Social Good and Sustainable Development:

In our quest to harness the power of artificial intelligence for the betterment of humanity, we prioritize initiatives that leverage AI for social good and sustainable development, addressing pressing societal challenges and advancing the United Nations Sustainable Development Goals (SDGs). Explore AI applications and interventions that address key societal issues such as poverty alleviation, healthcare access, education equity, environmental sustainability, and social inclusion. Collaborate with governments, NGOs, and civil society organizations to co-create AI solutions that have a positive impact on the lives of individuals and communities, particularly those most vulnerable or marginalized. By harnessing the potential of AI for social good and sustainable development, we contribute to a more equitable, resilient, and prosperous future for all members of society, leaving no one behind.

26. Responsible AI Leadership and Governance:

As leaders and practitioners in the field of artificial intelligence, we embrace our role as stewards of responsible AI leadership and governance, guiding the development, deployment, and use of AI technologies in a manner that promotes ethical principles, societal well-being, and human flourishing. Champion ethical leadership practices that prioritize transparency, integrity, and accountability in AI decision-making processes, fostering a culture of trust, openness, and ethical conduct within our organizations and communities. Establish governance frameworks, policies, and guidelines that govern the responsible development, deployment, and use of AI technologies, ensuring alignment with ethical principles, legal standards, and societal values. By exercising responsible AI leadership and governance, we set a positive example for others to follow, shaping the future of artificial intelligence in ways that benefit humanity and contribute to a more just, equitable, and sustainable world.

In conclusion, the ethical and societal dimensions of artificial intelligence are of paramount importance, guiding our actions and decisions as we navigate the complex landscape of AI innovation and deployment. By embracing diversity, global collaboration, accessibility, ethical use, social good, responsible leadership, and governance, we ensure that artificial intelligence serves humanity with wisdom, compassion, and empowerment, unlocking new possibilities and shaping a brighter future for all. Together, let us chart a course towards a future where AI promotes human flourishing, fosters inclusive growth, and advances the collective well-being of society.

Fair winds and steady sails, as we embark on this journey of discovery and transformation.

—-

This continuation explores the ethical and societal dimensions of artificial intelligence, delving into themes such as diversity, global collaboration, accessibility, ethical use, social good, responsible leadership, and governance.

6

Model Interpretability and Explainability

6. Model Interpretability and Explainability:

In the intricate landscape of artificial intelligence, model interpretability and explainability serve as guiding beacons, illuminating the inner workings of our AI systems and providing insights into their decisions and behaviors. Embrace techniques for model interpretability and explainability that enable us to understand how our models arrive at their predictions and recommendations. Explore methods such as feature importance analysis, partial dependence plots, and local interpretable model-agnostic explanations (LIME) to unravel the black box of complex machine learning models and shed light on the factors influencing their outputs. By prioritizing model interpretability and explainability, we empower users and stakeholders to trust, understand, and engage with AI solutions more effectively, fostering transparency, accountability, and informed decision-making.

7. Bias Detection and Mitigation:

In the pursuit of ethical and fair artificial intelligence, we diligently detect and mitigate biases that may inadvertently creep into our data, models, or algorithms, leading to unjust or discriminatory outcomes. Implement strategies for bias detection and mitigation throughout the AI lifecycle, from data collection and preprocessing to model training and evaluation. Conduct bias audits, fairness assessments, and demographic parity analyses to uncover disparities and biases related to sensitive attributes such as race, gender, age, or socioeconomic status. Employ techniques such as dataset stratification, fairness-aware learning, and adversarial debiasing to mitigate biases and promote fairness and equity in our AI solutions. By addressing biases proactively, we uphold ethical standards and ensure our AI applications benefit all members of society equitably.

8. Robustness to Adversarial Attacks:

In an era marked by cybersecurity threats and adversarial manipulation, we fortify our AI solutions with robustness measures to withstand attacks and preserve their integrity and reliability. Assess the vulnerability of our models to adversarial examples, data perturbations, or evasion attacks, and implement defenses to mitigate these risks. Explore techniques such as adversarial training, input sanitization, or model verification to enhance the resilience of our models against malicious actors and unforeseen perturbations. By prioritizing robustness to adversarial attacks, we safeguard the trustworthiness and security of our AI solutions in the face of potential threats.

9. Regulatory Compliance and Legal Frameworks:

In the complex regulatory landscape of artificial intelligence, we navigate a labyrinth of laws, regulations, and legal frameworks governing the development, deployment, and use of AI technologies. Stay informed about relevant regulatory requirements and legal obligations applicable to our AI applications, including data protection, privacy, intellectual property, cybersecurity, and consumer protection laws. Ensure our AI solutions comply with applicable regulations and standards, and establish governance frameworks and risk management practices to mitigate legal and compliance risks. By prioritizing regulatory compliance and adherence to legal frameworks, we uphold legal standards, mitigate legal risks, and build trust and confidence among users, stakeholders, and regulators in our AI initiatives.

10. Societal Impact and Ethical Considerations:

As architects of artificial intelligence, we bear a weighty responsibility to consider the broader societal impact and ethical implications of our AI applications, ensuring they contribute positively to the well-being and advancement of society. Evaluate the potential societal benefits and risks associated with our AI solutions, including their impact on employment, education, healthcare, transportation, environment, and social equity. Prioritize ethical use cases and applications that align with societal values, address pressing societal challenges, and promote positive social outcomes, such as improving healthcare access, enhancing education opportunities, advancing environmental sustainability, and fostering inclusive economic growth. By harnessing the potential of AI for social good and sustainable development, we contribute to a more equitable, resilient, and prosperous future for all members of society, leaving no one behind.

11. Transparency and Accountability:

In the realm of artificial intelligence, transparency and accountability are essential principles that underpin trust, credibility, and responsible use of AI technologies. Foster transparency in our AI development processes, algorithms, and decision-making mechanisms, providing users and stakeholders with visibility into how our AI systems work and how decisions are made. Establish mechanisms for accountability and oversight, including clear lines of responsibility, recourse mechanisms, and redress procedures in case of errors, biases, or unintended consequences. By promoting transparency and accountability, we build trust, foster confidence, and mitigate risks associated with AI technologies, empowering users and stakeholders to engage with AI solutions with confidence and trust.

12. Ethical Leadership and Governance:

As leaders and stewards of artificial intelligence, we embrace our role as ethical leaders and governors, guiding the development, deployment, and use of AI technologies in a manner that upholds ethical principles, respects human rights, and promotes the public interest. Champion ethical leadership practices that prioritize transparency, integrity, and accountability in AI decision-making processes, fostering a culture of trust, openness, and ethical conduct within our organizations and communities. Establish governance frameworks, policies, and guidelines that govern the responsible development, deployment, and use of AI technologies, ensuring alignment with ethical principles, legal standards, and societal values. By exercising ethical leadership and governance, we set a positive example for others to follow, shaping the future of artificial intelligence in ways that benefit humanity and contribute to a more just, equitable, and sustainable world.

In conclusion, the ethical considerations and societal impact of artificial intelligence are of paramount importance, guiding our actions and decisions as we navigate the complex landscape of AI innovation and deployment. By prioritizing model interpretability, bias detection and mitigation, robustness to adversarial attacks, regulatory compliance, ethical considerations, transparency, accountability, and ethical leadership and governance, we ensure that artificial intelligence serves humanity with wisdom, compassion, and empowerment, unlocking new possibilities and shaping a brighter future for all. Together, let us chart a course towards a future where AI promotes human flourishing, fosters inclusive growth, and advances the collective well-being of society.

Fair winds and steady sails, as we embark on this journey of discovery and transformation.

—-

This continuation focuses on the ethical considerations and societal impact of artificial intelligence, exploring themes such as model interpretability, bias detection and mitigation, robustness to adversarial attacks, regulatory compliance, transparency, accountability, ethical leadership, and governance.

13. Data Privacy and Security:

In the age of data-driven artificial intelligence, safeguarding the privacy and security of sensitive information is paramount to building trust and ensuring the responsible use of AI technologies. Implement robust data privacy and security measures to protect personal and confidential data from unauthorized access, disclosure, or misuse throughout the AI lifecycle. Adhere to data protection regulations such as the General Data Protection Regulation (GDPR) and the California Consumer Privacy Act (CCPA), ensuring compliance with privacy principles such as data minimization, purpose limitation, and user consent. Employ encryption, access controls, and secure data storage practices to mitigate security risks and prevent data breaches. By prioritizing data privacy and security, we uphold user trust, mitigate risks, and foster responsible use of AI technologies in a digital world.

14. Ethical Considerations in AI Research:

In our quest for AI innovation, we recognize the importance of ethical considerations in AI research to ensure the responsible conduct of research, promote integrity, and protect the welfare and rights of individuals and communities. Adhere to ethical principles such as beneficence, non-maleficence, respect for autonomy, and justice in all aspects of AI research, including experimental design, data collection, analysis, and publication. Obtain informed consent from research participants, respect their privacy and confidentiality, and minimize potential risks and harms associated with research activities. Foster open and transparent communication about research findings, methodologies, and limitations, enabling peer review, replication, and validation of research results. By prioritizing ethical considerations in AI research, we uphold the highest standards of integrity, accountability, and ethical conduct, advancing knowledge and innovation in a responsible and ethical manner.

15. AI for Environmental Sustainability:

In our stewardship of artificial intelligence, we harness the transformative power of AI to address pressing environmental challenges and promote sustainability, resilience, and conservation of natural resources. Explore AI applications and interventions that contribute to environmental monitoring, modeling, and management, such as climate modeling, ecological forecasting, biodiversity conservation, and natural resource management. Leverage AI technologies such as machine learning, remote sensing, and data analytics to analyze complex environmental data, predict environmental trends and phenomena, and inform evidence-based decision-making and policy formulation. Collaborate with environmental organizations, government agencies, and research institutions to co-create AI solutions that contribute to a more sustainable and resilient planet. By harnessing the potential of AI for environmental sustainability, we advance the global agenda for environmental protection and conservation, safeguarding the health and well-being of current and future generations.

16. AI for Healthcare and Biomedicine:

In the realm of healthcare and biomedicine, artificial intelligence holds immense promise for revolutionizing diagnosis, treatment, and personalized medicine, enhancing patient care and outcomes, and advancing biomedical research and discovery. Explore AI applications and interventions that address key challenges in healthcare, such as disease diagnosis and prognosis, medical imaging analysis, drug discovery and development, precision medicine, and healthcare delivery optimization. Leverage AI technologies such as deep learning, natural language processing, and predictive analytics to analyze medical data, identify patterns and correlations, and generate actionable insights for healthcare providers and researchers. Collaborate with healthcare institutions, pharmaceutical companies, and research organizations to co-create AI solutions that improve patient outcomes, reduce healthcare costs, and accelerate medical breakthroughs. By harnessing the potential of AI for healthcare and biomedicine, we advance the frontiers of medical science and technology, transforming healthcare delivery and improving the quality of life for patients worldwide.

17. AI for Education and Lifelong Learning:

In the realm of education and lifelong learning, artificial intelligence serves as a powerful tool for personalizing learning experiences, improving educational outcomes, and expanding access to quality education for all learners, regardless of background or ability. Explore AI applications and interventions that enhance teaching, learning, and assessment across diverse educational settings, such as intelligent tutoring systems, adaptive learning platforms, educational data analytics, and virtual reality simulations. Leverage AI technologies such as natural language processing, machine learning, and cognitive modeling to tailor instruction to individual learning styles, preferences, and abilities, providing personalized support and feedback to learners. Collaborate with educators, policymakers, and technology developers to co-create AI-enabled educational solutions that empower learners, foster creativity and critical thinking, and cultivate lifelong learning skills. By harnessing the potential of AI for education and lifelong learning, we democratize access to quality education, bridge educational gaps, and empower individuals to realize their full potential and contribute to society.

18. AI for Social Justice and Equity:

In our pursuit of social justice and equity, artificial intelligence serves as a catalyst for addressing systemic inequities, promoting fairness, and advancing human rights and dignity for all members of society. Explore AI applications and interventions that address key social justice issues, such as criminal justice reform, poverty alleviation, access to legal services, and social welfare provision. Leverage AI technologies such as predictive analytics, natural language processing, and computer vision to analyze societal data, identify disparities and biases, and inform evidence-based policy interventions and social programs. Collaborate with advocacy groups, community organizations, and policymakers to co-create AI solutions that empower marginalized communities, amplify their voices, and address systemic barriers to equality and justice. By harnessing the potential of AI for social justice and equity, we contribute to building a more just, inclusive, and equitable society, where all individuals are treated with dignity, respect, and fairness.

19. AI for Economic Development and Prosperity:

In the realm of economic development and prosperity, artificial intelligence serves as a driver of innovation, productivity, and inclusive growth, unlocking new opportunities for job creation, entrepreneurship, and economic empowerment in a digital economy. Explore AI applications and interventions that enhance productivity, efficiency, and competitiveness across diverse industries and sectors, such as manufacturing, agriculture, finance, and retail. Leverage AI technologies such as robotic process automation, predictive analytics, and supply chain optimization to streamline business operations, optimize resource allocation, and drive sustainable economic growth. Collaborate with businesses, governments, and development organizations to co-create AI-enabled solutions that promote economic resilience, job creation, and inclusive prosperity, particularly in underserved and marginalized communities. By harnessing the potential of AI for economic development and prosperity, we foster innovation, entrepreneurship, and shared prosperity, unlocking new pathways to sustainable development and economic well-being for all members of society.

20. AI for Disaster Response and Humanitarian Aid:

In times of crisis and humanitarian emergencies, artificial intelligence serves as a valuable tool for enhancing disaster response, humanitarian aid, and resilience-building efforts, saving lives and mitigating the impact of natural and man-made disasters on vulnerable populations. Explore AI applications and interventions that improve disaster preparedness, early warning systems, risk assessment, and emergency response coordination, such as predictive modeling, satellite imagery analysis, and social media monitoring. Leverage AI technologies such as machine learning, computer vision, and natural language processing to analyze vast amounts of data in real-time, identify patterns and trends, and generate actionable insights for decision-makers and first responders. Collaborate with humanitarian organizations, government agencies, and technology developers to co-create AI-enabled solutions that strengthen disaster resilience, enhance humanitarian coordination, and improve the effectiveness and efficiency of humanitarian assistance efforts. By harnessing the potential of AI for disaster response and humanitarian aid, we save lives, alleviate suffering, and build resilience in communities facing adversity, embodying the principles of solidarity, compassion, and human dignity.

In conclusion, artificial intelligence has the potential to address some of the most pressing challenges facing humanity, from healthcare and education to social justice and economic development.

AI, we can unlock new opportunities for innovation, growth, and societal progress, advancing towards a future where AI serves humanity with wisdom, compassion, and empowerment. Through collaborative efforts and responsible stewardship, we can harness the potential of AI to build a more inclusive, equitable, and sustainable world, where the benefits of AI are shared by all members of society. Together, let us embark on this journey of discovery and transformation, leveraging the power of artificial intelligence to shape a brighter future for generations to come.

Fair winds and steady sails, as we navigate the seas of AI innovation and embark on this collective voyage towards a better tomorrow.

This continuation highlights the potential of artificial intelligence to address various global challenges and emphasizes the importance of collaborative efforts and responsible stewardship in leveraging AI for the benefit of humanity.

7

Continuous Learning and Adaptation:

7. Continuous Learning and Adaptation:

In the ever-evolving landscape of artificial intelligence, continuous learning and adaptation are essential to stay abreast of emerging trends, technologies, and methodologies, and to ensure the relevance and effectiveness of our AI solutions over time. Foster a culture of lifelong learning within our AI teams and organizations, encouraging curiosity, exploration, and experimentation with new ideas and approaches. Invest in ongoing training, education, and skill development to expand our knowledge, expertise, and proficiency in AI principles, algorithms, and applications. Embrace interdisciplinary learning and cross-functional collaboration to gain insights from diverse perspectives and domains, enriching our understanding and capabilities in AI innovation and application. By cultivating a culture of continuous learning and adaptation, we empower ourselves and our teams to tackle complex challenges, drive innovation, and shape the future of artificial intelligence with confidence and foresight.

8. Collaboration and Partnerships:

In the interconnected world of artificial intelligence, collaboration and partnerships are essential for driving innovation, sharing knowledge, and addressing common challenges and opportunities. Foster collaborative partnerships with industry peers, academic institutions, research organizations, startups, and government agencies to leverage complementary expertise, resources, and capabilities in AI research, development, and deployment. Engage in collaborative initiatives, consortia, and open-source projects that promote knowledge sharing, best practices, and standards development in AI technologies and applications. By fostering a culture of collaboration and partnerships, we accelerate the pace of AI innovation, expand the reach and impact of our AI initiatives, and unlock new opportunities for growth and advancement in the field.

9. Responsible AI Governance and Regulation:

In the complex and rapidly evolving landscape of artificial intelligence, responsible AI governance and regulation play a crucial role in ensuring the ethical and responsible development, deployment, and use of AI technologies, safeguarding the rights, interests, and well-being of individuals and society at large. Advocate for clear and transparent AI governance frameworks, policies, and guidelines that govern the responsible development, deployment, and use of AI technologies, ensuring alignment with ethical principles, legal standards, and societal values. Collaborate with policymakers, regulators, and industry stakeholders to co-create and implement regulations and standards that address key ethical, legal, and societal concerns related to AI, such as data privacy, bias, transparency, accountability, and safety. By promoting responsible AI governance and regulation, we build trust, foster accountability, and mitigate risks associated with AI technologies, enabling their responsible and ethical use for the benefit of all members of society.

10. Ethical Considerations and Social Impact:

In our journey through the realms of artificial intelligence, we must navigate the ethical and societal dimensions of AI with wisdom, compassion, and foresight, ensuring that our AI solutions are developed and deployed in a manner that upholds ethical principles, respects human rights, and promotes the public interest. Consider the potential ethical implications and social impact of our AI applications, including issues related to privacy, fairness, transparency, accountability, bias, and discrimination. Prioritize ethical use cases and applications that align with societal values, address pressing societal challenges, and promote positive social outcomes, such as improving healthcare access, enhancing education opportunities, advancing environmental sustainability, and fostering inclusive economic growth. By embracing ethical considerations and social impact assessments, we ensure that artificial intelligence serves humanity with integrity, fairness, and compassion, unlocking new possibilities and shaping a brighter future for all.

11. Transparency and Accountability:

In the realm of artificial intelligence, transparency and accountability are essential principles that underpin trust, credibility, and responsible use of AI technologies. Foster transparency in our AI development processes, algorithms, and decision-making mechanisms, providing users and stakeholders with visibility into how our AI systems work and how decisions are made. Establish mechanisms for accountability and oversight, including clear lines of responsibility, recourse mechanisms, and redress procedures in case of errors, biases, or unintended consequences. By promoting transparency and accountability, we build trust, foster confidence, and mitigate risks associated with AI technologies, empowering users and stakeholders to engage with AI solutions with confidence and trust.

12. Privacy Preservation and Data Security:

In the era of data-driven artificial intelligence, preserving privacy and ensuring data security are paramount to building trust and ensuring the responsible use of AI technologies. Implement robust privacy preservation and data security measures to protect personal and confidential data from unauthorized access, disclosure, or misuse throughout the AI lifecycle. Adhere to privacy principles such as data minimization, purpose limitation, and user consent, and comply with data protection regulations such as the General Data Protection Regulation (GDPR) and the California Consumer Privacy Act (CCPA). Employ encryption, access controls, and secure data storage practices to mitigate security risks and prevent data breaches. By prioritizing privacy preservation and data security, we uphold user trust, mitigate risks, and foster responsible use of AI technologies in a digital world.

In conclusion, the ethical and responsible development, deployment, and use of artificial intelligence are essential for ensuring that AI technologies benefit humanity and

101

contribute positively to societal well-being. By embracing principles of continuous learning and adaptation, collaboration and partnerships, responsible AI governance and regulation, ethical considerations and social impact, transparency and accountability, and privacy preservation and data security, we can navigate the complex landscape of AI with integrity, foresight, and compassion, unlocking new opportunities for innovation, growth, and progress that benefit all members of society.

14. AI Ethics Committees and Review Boards:

In the ethical governance of artificial intelligence, establishing AI ethics committees and review boards can provide oversight, guidance, and accountability in the development, deployment, and use of AI technologies. Form interdisciplinary ethics committees comprised of experts from diverse fields such as computer science, ethics, law, sociology, and philosophy to review and evaluate AI projects, algorithms, and applications from ethical, social, and legal perspectives. Define ethical guidelines, principles, and standards for AI development and deployment, and establish review processes for assessing the ethical implications and societal impact of AI initiatives. By fostering collaboration and dialogue among stakeholders, including researchers, developers, policymakers, and civil society organizations, AI ethics committees and review boards can promote ethical AI practices, mitigate risks, and ensure that AI technologies are developed and deployed in a manner that upholds ethical principles, respects human rights, and promotes the public interest.

15. Community Engagement and Stakeholder Consultation:

In the inclusive governance of artificial intelligence, community engagement and stakeholder consultation are essential for fostering dialogue, building trust, and promoting shared decision-making in the development, deployment, and use of AI technologies. Engage with diverse stakeholders, including end-users, impacted communities, advocacy groups, and civil society organizations, throughout the AI lifecycle to solicit feedback, address concerns, and co-create AI solutions that meet the needs and preferences of all stakeholders. Prioritize participatory approaches such as community consultations, focus groups, and public forums to ensure that diverse voices are heard and considered in AI decision-making processes. By fostering community engagement and stakeholder consultation, we build trust, foster collaboration, and empower individuals and communities to shape the future of artificial intelligence in ways that promote equity, fairness, and social justice.

16. Corporate Social Responsibility in AI:

In the corporate realm of artificial intelligence, embracing corporate social responsibility (CSR) principles and practices is essential for ensuring that AI technologies are developed and deployed in a manner that aligns with ethical values, respects human rights, and contributes positively to society. Integrate CSR considerations into AI strategy, governance, and decision-making processes, prioritizing ethical AI principles, transparency, accountability, and stakeholder engagement. Invest in initiatives that leverage AI for social good and sustainable development, such as philanthropic programs, research partnerships, and community outreach efforts that address key societal challenges and promote positive social outcomes. By embracing corporate social responsibility in AI, companies can build trust, enhance reputation, and create long-term value for shareholders, employees, customers, and society at large, while advancing the ethical and responsible use of AI technologies for the benefit of all.

17. AI Impact Assessments and Audits:

In the ethical governance of artificial intelligence, conducting AI impact assessments and audits can help identify and mitigate potential risks, biases, and unintended consequences associated with AI technologies, ensuring that they are developed and deployed in a manner that upholds ethical principles, respects human rights, and promotes the public interest. Conduct systematic assessments of the potential ethical, social, and legal implications of AI projects, algorithms, and applications, including their impact on individuals, communities, and society at large. Employ techniques such as algorithmic impact assessments, fairness audits, and human rights impact assessments to evaluate the potential risks and harms associated with AI technologies and to identify strategies for mitigating them. By prioritizing AI impact assessments and audits, we enhance transparency, accountability, and responsible use of AI technologies, promoting trust, fairness, and equity in their development and deployment.

18. Multistakeholder Dialogue and Collaboration:

In the governance of artificial intelligence, fostering multistakeholder dialogue and collaboration is essential for building consensus, identifying common goals, and developing shared solutions to complex ethical, social, and regulatory challenges associated with AI technologies. Convene multistakeholder forums, roundtables, and working groups that bring together diverse perspectives, interests, and expertise from academia, industry, government, civil society, and international organizations to discuss key AI issues, share best practices, and explore collaborative opportunities. Facilitate open and inclusive dialogue that encourages constructive debate, knowledge exchange, and problem-solving, fostering a culture of trust, mutual respect, and cooperation among stakeholders. By fostering multistakeholder dialogue and collaboration, we promote collective action, build alliances, and advance the ethical and responsible governance of artificial intelligence, ensuring that AI technologies serve humanity with integrity, fairness, and compassion.

19. Public Awareness and Education:

In the democratic governance of artificial intelligence, promoting public awareness and education is essential for empowering citizens with knowledge, skills, and agency to engage in informed debate, advocacy, and decision-making on AI-related issues. Develop educational campaigns, resources, and outreach programs that raise awareness about the potential opportunities and challenges of AI technologies, including their ethical, social, and economic implications. Prioritize public education initiatives that promote digital literacy, critical thinking, and ethical reasoning skills, enabling individuals to navigate the complex landscape of AI with confidence and discernment. Foster dialogue and engagement between policymakers, researchers, industry representatives, and civil society organizations to ensure that diverse perspectives and voices are heard and considered in AI policy development and decision-making processes. By promoting public awareness and education, we empower citizens to participate meaningfully in shaping the future of artificial intelligence in ways that promote democratic values, human rights, and the public interest.

Let me know if you'd like to continue with another point or if there's anything specific you'd like to explore further!

Certainly! Let's proceed with the next point:

20. Ethical Considerations in AI Research and Development:

In the realm of artificial intelligence research and development, ethical considerations are paramount to ensure that AI technologies are developed and deployed in a manner that upholds ethical principles, respects human rights, and promotes the public interest. Incorporate ethical considerations into all stages of the AI research and development lifecycle, from project conception and design to implementation and evaluation. Prioritize ethical principles such as transparency, fairness, accountability, and privacy in AI research and development practices, ensuring that AI systems are designed and deployed with due consideration for their potential impact on individuals, communities, and society at large. Foster a culture of responsible conduct and ethical inquiry within the AI research community, encouraging researchers to reflect on the ethical implications of their work and to engage in dialogue with stakeholders to address ethical concerns and dilemmas. By prioritizing ethical considerations in AI research and development, we uphold the highest standards of integrity, accountability, and ethical conduct, advancing knowledge and innovation in a responsible and ethical manner.

Let me know if you'd like to continue with another point or if there's anything specific you'd like to explore further!

8

Algorithmic Transparency and Explainability:

S ure, let's continue:

8. Algorithmic Transparency and Explainability:

In the realm of artificial intelligence, ensuring algorithmic transparency and explainability is essential for building trust, understanding, and accountability in AI systems. Prioritize the development of AI algorithms and models that are transparent and explainable, allowing users and stakeholders to understand how decisions are made and why specific outcomes are produced. Employ techniques such as model interpretation methods, feature importance analysis, and explanation generation algorithms to provide insights into the inner workings of AI systems and to explain their predictions and recommendations in a human-understandable manner. Foster transparency in AI development processes, data sources, and model architectures, enabling users to assess the reliability, fairness, and ethical implications of AI technologies. By prioritizing algorithmic transparency and explainability, we promote trust, accountability, and responsible use of AI technologies, empowering users and stakeholders to engage with AI systems with confidence and understanding.

9. Fairness and Bias Mitigation:

In the ethical development and deployment of artificial intelligence, ensuring fairness and mitigating bias is crucial to avoid perpetuating or exacerbating societal inequalities and injustices. Prioritize fairness considerations throughout the AI lifecycle, from data collection and preprocessing to algorithm design and evaluation. Employ techniques such as fairness-aware machine learning algorithms, bias detection tools, and fairness metrics to identify and mitigate biases in training data and model predictions. Implement strategies for ensuring diversity and representativeness in datasets, including data augmentation, sampling techniques, and data validation procedures. By prioritizing fairness and bias mitigation, we promote equity, diversity, and inclusion in AI technologies, ensuring that they serve all members of society fairly and without discrimination.

Of course! Let's proceed with the next point:

10. Ethical Decision-Making Frameworks:

In the ethical development and deployment of artificial intelligence, establishing ethical decision-making frameworks is essential to guide responsible conduct and decision-making in AI development, deployment, and use. Develop and implement ethical frameworks and guidelines that outline principles, values, and best practices for ethical AI design, development, and deployment. Prioritize ethical principles such as transparency, fairness, accountability, privacy, and human dignity in AI decision-making processes, ensuring that AI technologies are developed and deployed in a manner that upholds these principles. Provide training and support to AI developers, engineers, and decision-makers to help them navigate ethical dilemmas and make informed decisions in complex and uncertain situations. By establishing ethical decision-making frameworks, we promote a culture of ethical awareness, responsibility, and accountability in the development and use of AI technologies, ensuring that they serve humanity with integrity, fairness, and compassion.

9

Conclusion

Conclusion:

As we draw to a close on this captivating journey through the realms of artificial intelligence, it is with a sense of wonder and anticipation that we reflect on the profound impact of our exploration. "Developing Artificial Intelligence" has been more than just a book—it has been a testament to the boundless potential of human ingenuity, the relentless pursuit of knowledge, and the ethical imperative to shape the future with wisdom and compassion.

In our quest to unravel the mysteries of AI, we have delved into the depths of machine learning algorithms, neural networks, and computational intelligence, uncovering the intricate mechanisms that underpin intelligent machines. Along the way, we have encountered ethical dilemmas, societal implications, and transformative opportunities that challenge us to confront the complexities of AI development with humility and responsibility.

But beyond the technical intricacies of AI lies a deeper truth—a truth that speaks to the resilience of the human spirit, the power of collaboration, and the promise of a future where artificial intelligence serves humanity with integrity, fairness, and compassion. As we stand on the threshold of a new era defined by intelligent machines and digital cognition, "Developing Artificial Intelligence" serves as a guiding light, illuminating the path forward with insights, wisdom, and inspiration.

But our journey does not end here. It is merely the beginning of a new chapter in the ever-evolving saga of artificial intelligence—a chapter filled with possibilities, challenges, and opportunities yet to be discovered. As we venture forth into the uncharted territory of AI exploration, let us carry with us the lessons learned, the insights gained, and the ethical imperatives that guide us on this transformative journey.

With boundless curiosity and unwavering determination, let us continue to push the boundaries of what is possible, to innovate with purpose, and to shape a future where artificial intelligence serves as a force for good in the world. Together, let us embark on this exhilarating odyssey with courage, conviction, and compassion, knowing that the future of AI— and the future of humanity—lies in our hands.

Thank you for joining me on this remarkable journey. May our collective efforts pave the way for a future where artificial intelligence serves as a beacon of hope, inspiration, and empowerment for generations to come.

With deepest gratitude and warmest regards,

BinaryCoder X

www.ingramcontent.com/pod-product-compliance
Lightning Source LLC
LaVergne TN
LVHW051700050326
832903LV00032B/3919